this book belongs to

_____

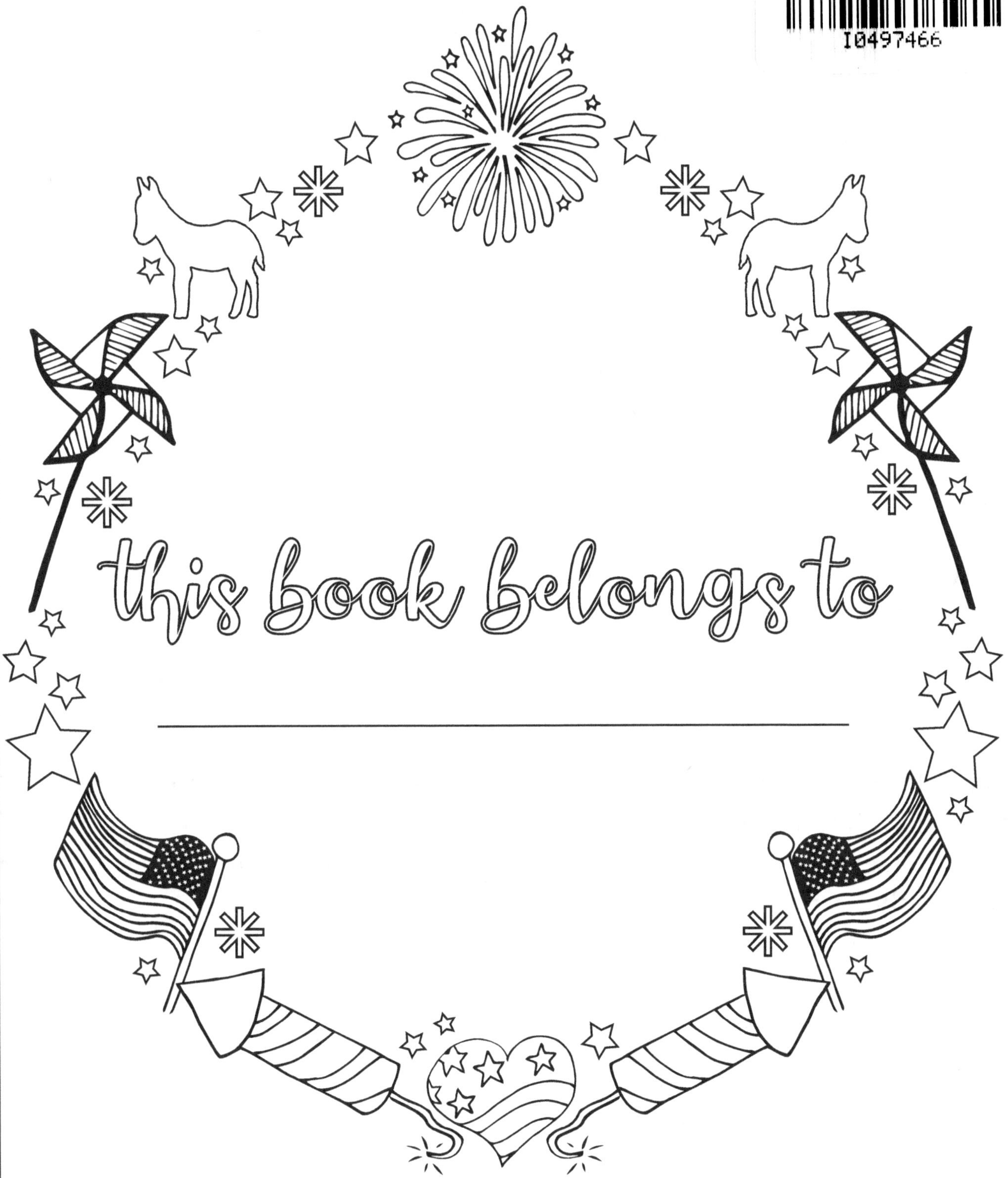

Copyright © 2020 Donkey Vote Press

Illustrated by Elizabeth Beeson

All rights reserved. No part of this book may be reproduced or transmitted in any form or by any means whatsoever without express written permission from the author, except in the case of reviews. Please refer all pertinent questions to the publisher.

This book features the following fonts:
Autery - Designer: Muhammad Naufal Anis
Cardenio Modern - Designer: Nils Cords
Subscriber - Designer: Alit Design
Big Snow - Designer: Syafrizal a.k.a. Khurasan
Nixie One - Designer: Jovanny Lemonad
Crafty Lover
Black Signature
Jost

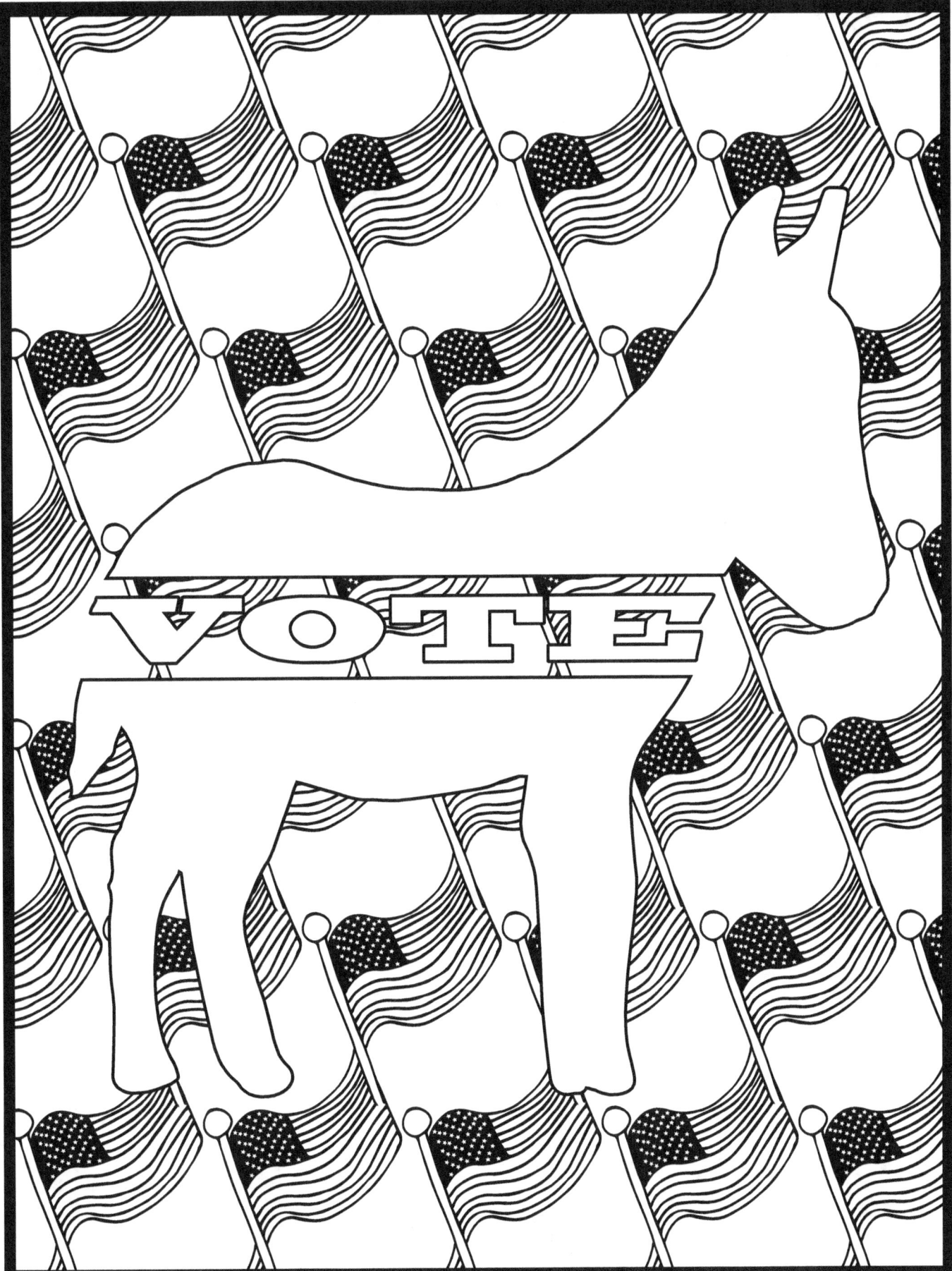

Donkey Vote

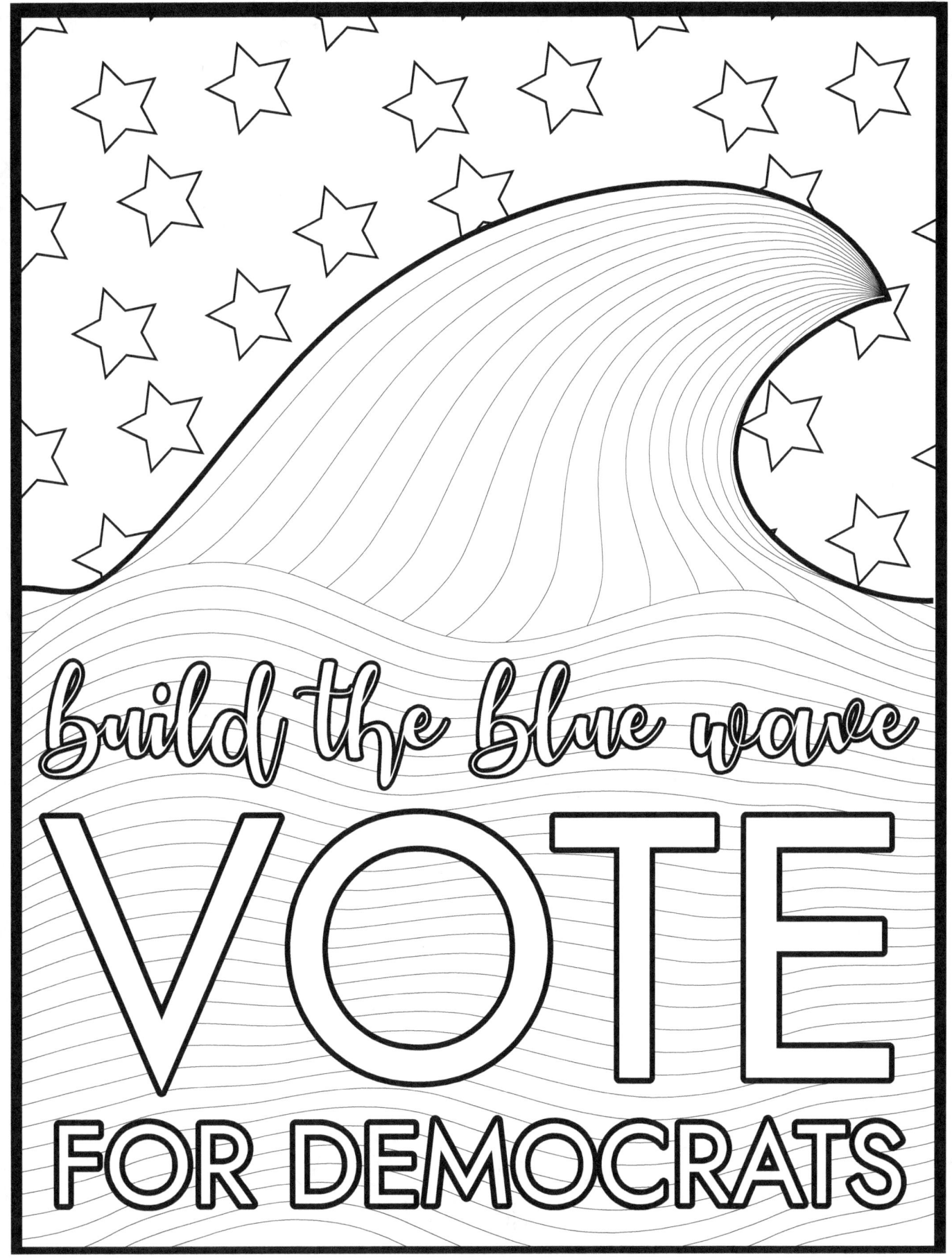

Blue Wave

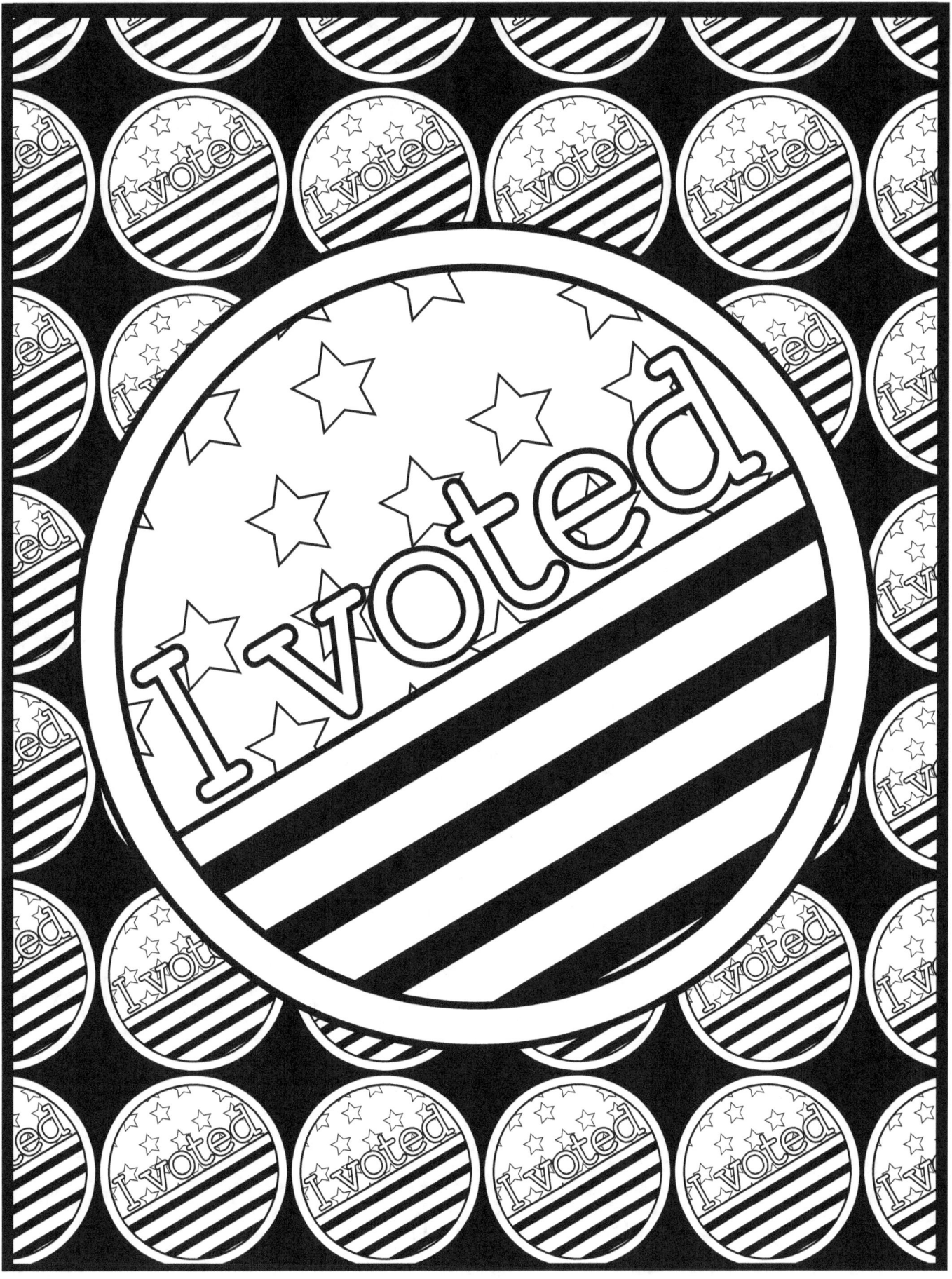

I VOTED

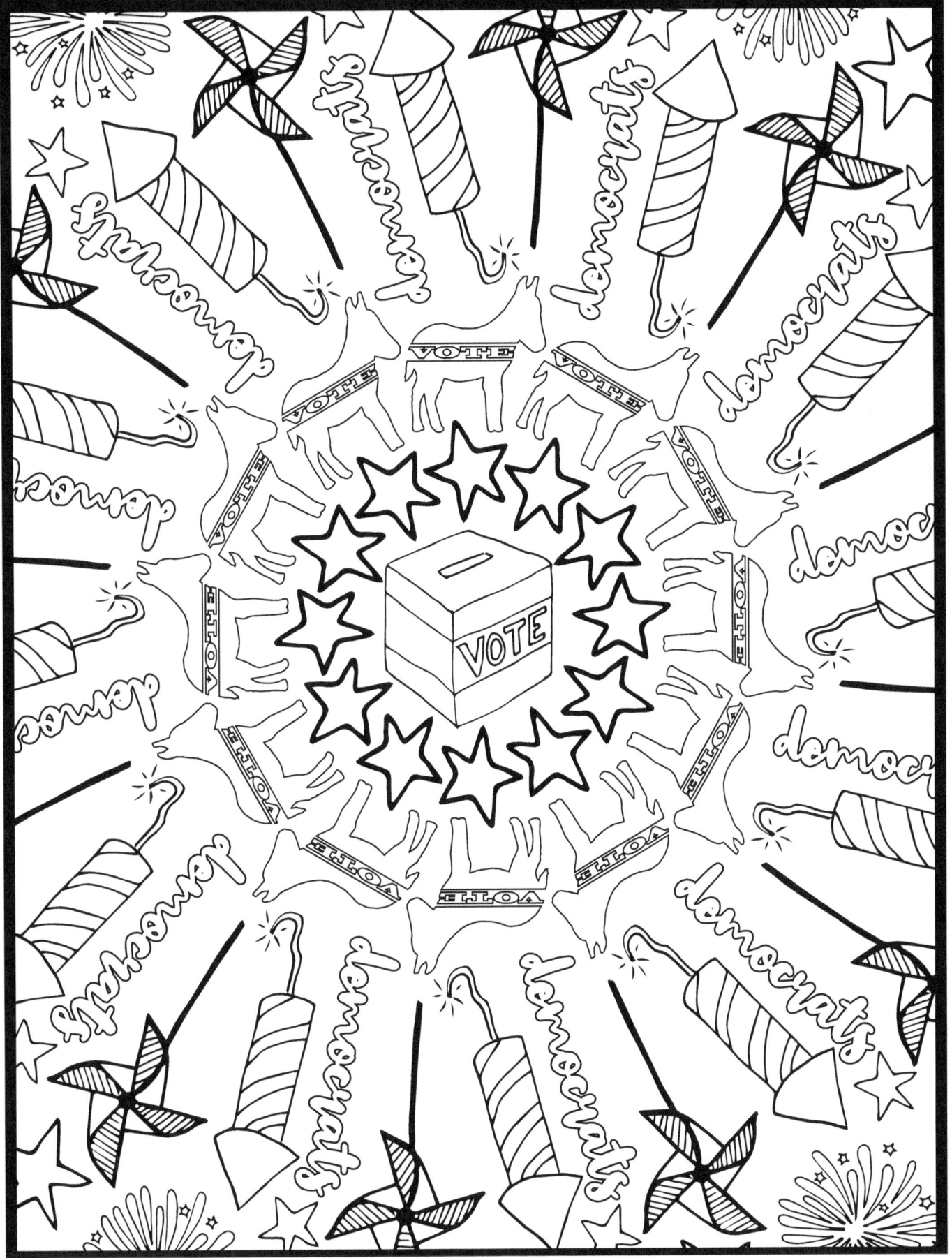

Democrats mandala

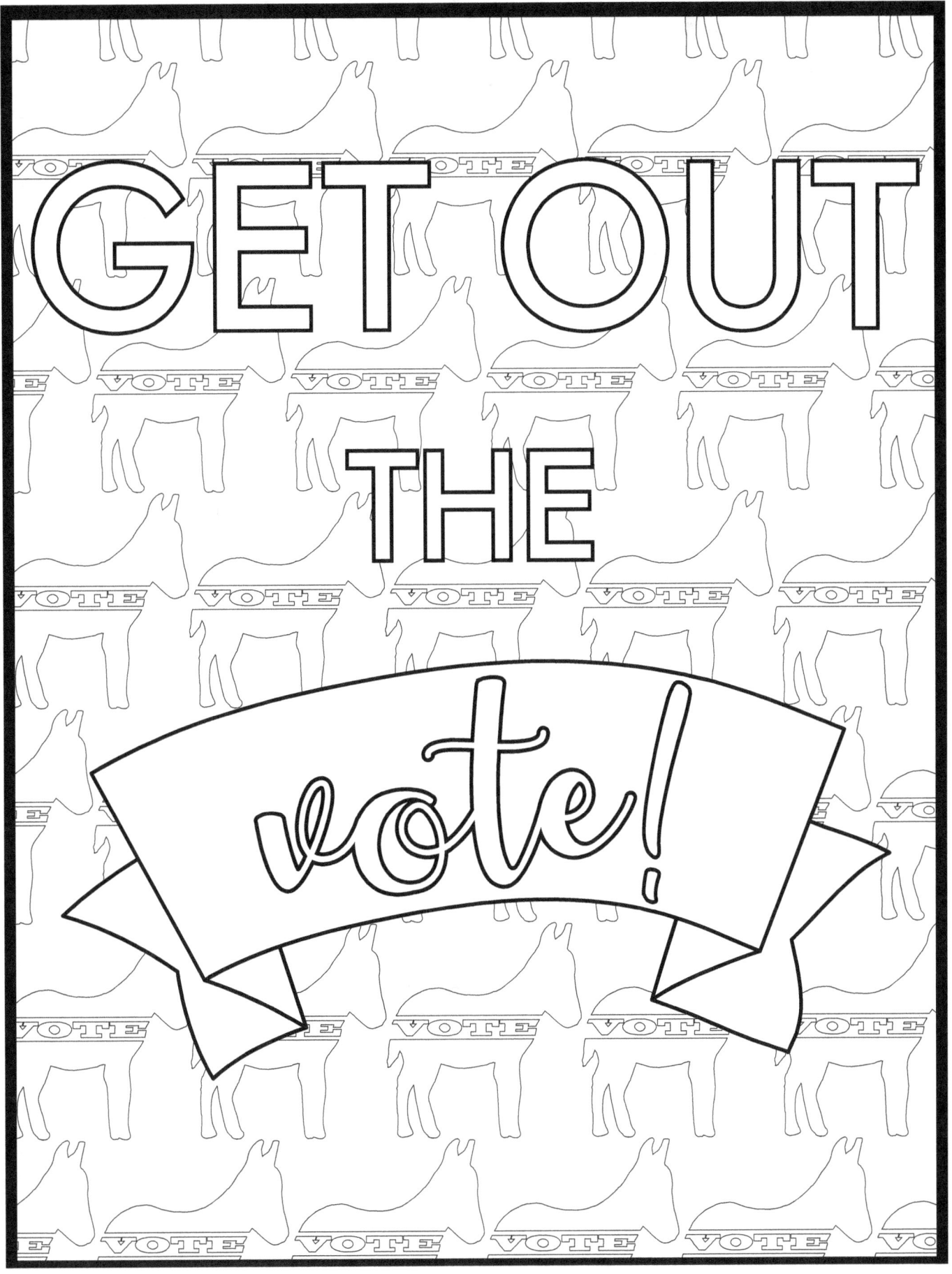

GET OUT THE VOTE!

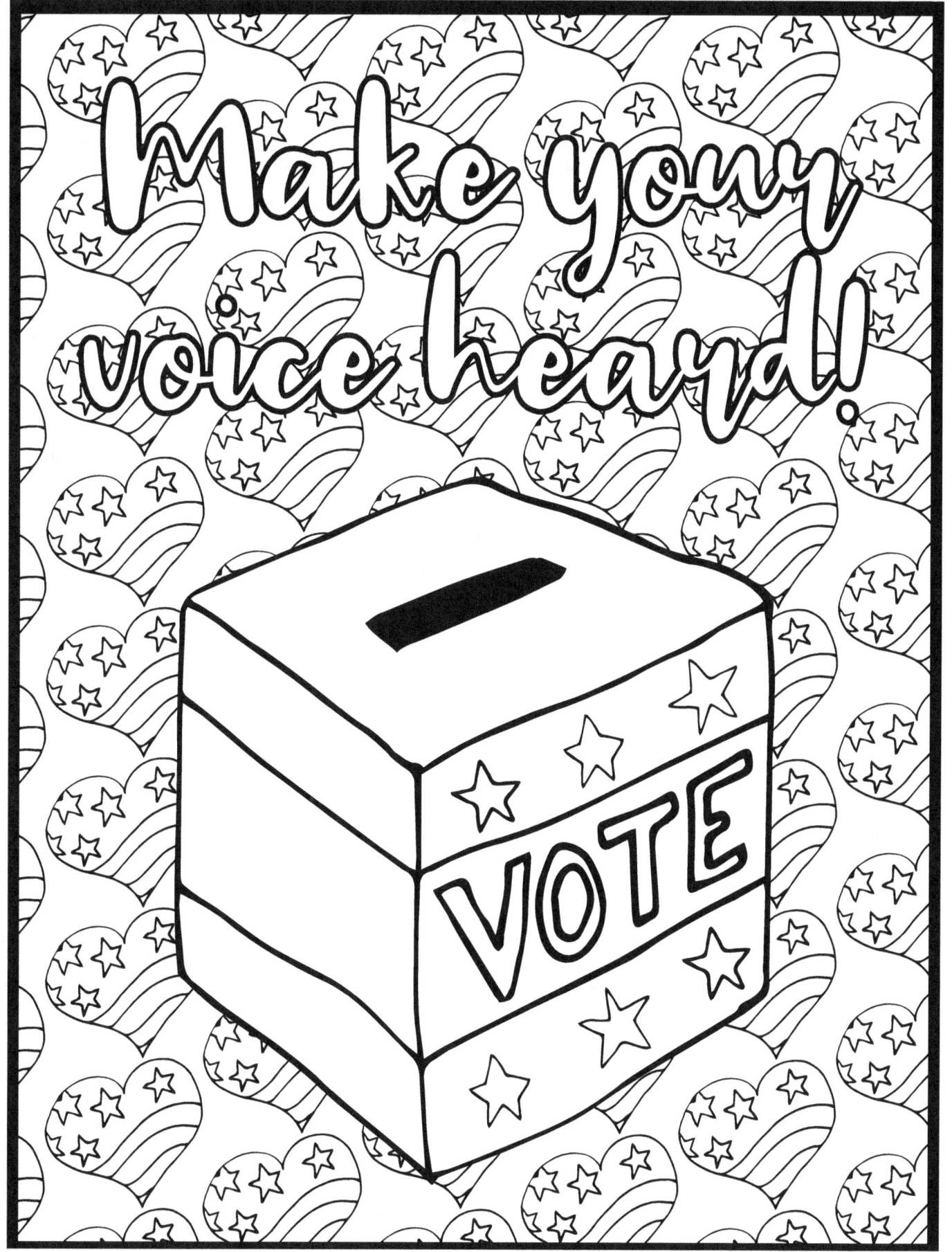

Make your voice heard!

By the people and for the people!

By the people and for the people!

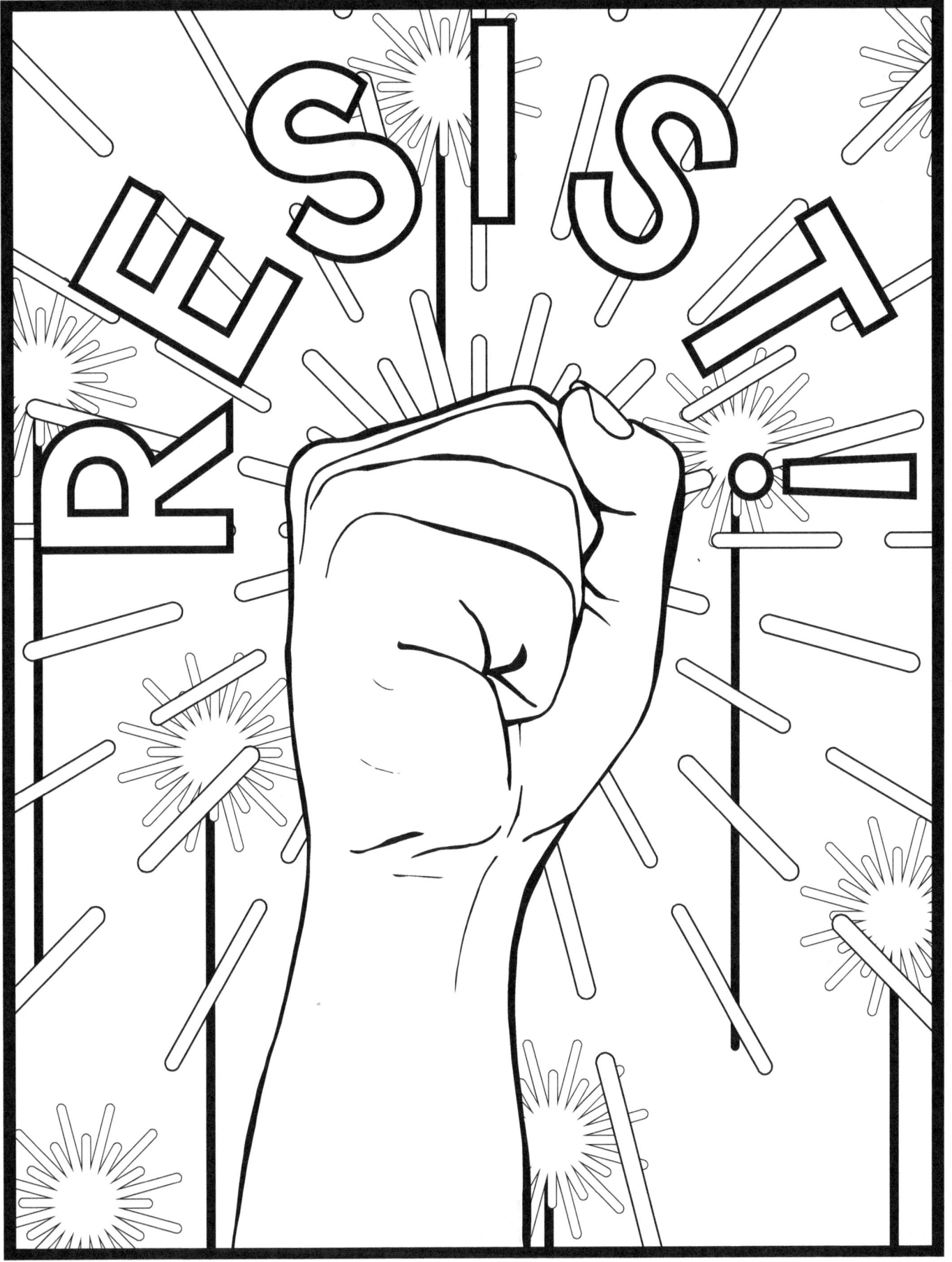

RESIST!

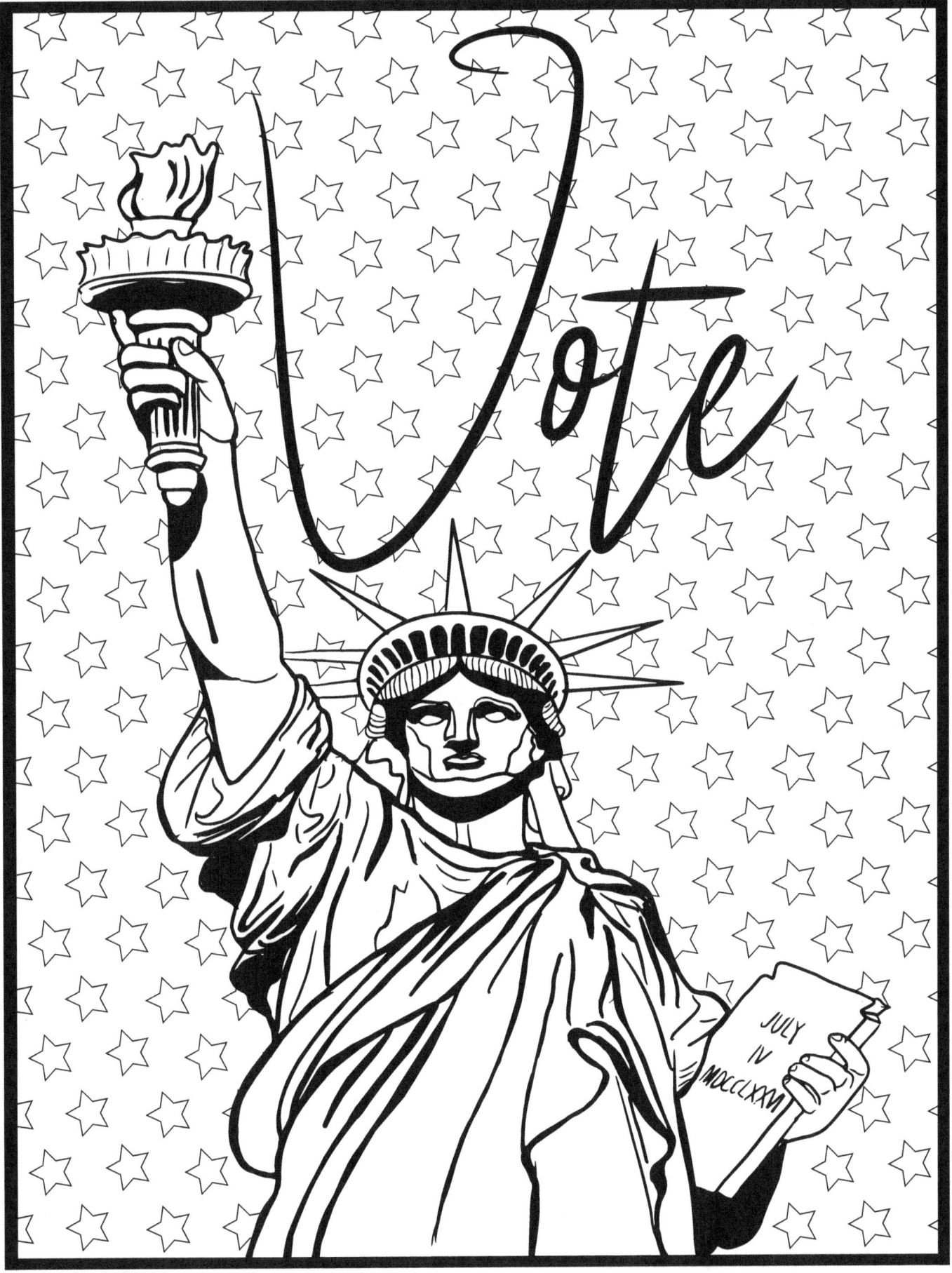

Lady Liberty

VOTE DEMOCRATIC

because

BLACK LIVES MATTER

women's rights are human rights

LOVE is LOVE

HEALTHCARE IS A HUMAN RIGHT

public education should stay public

workers deserve a living wage

corporations are NOT people

SCIENCE is REAL

gun violence must come to an end

Vote Democratic because

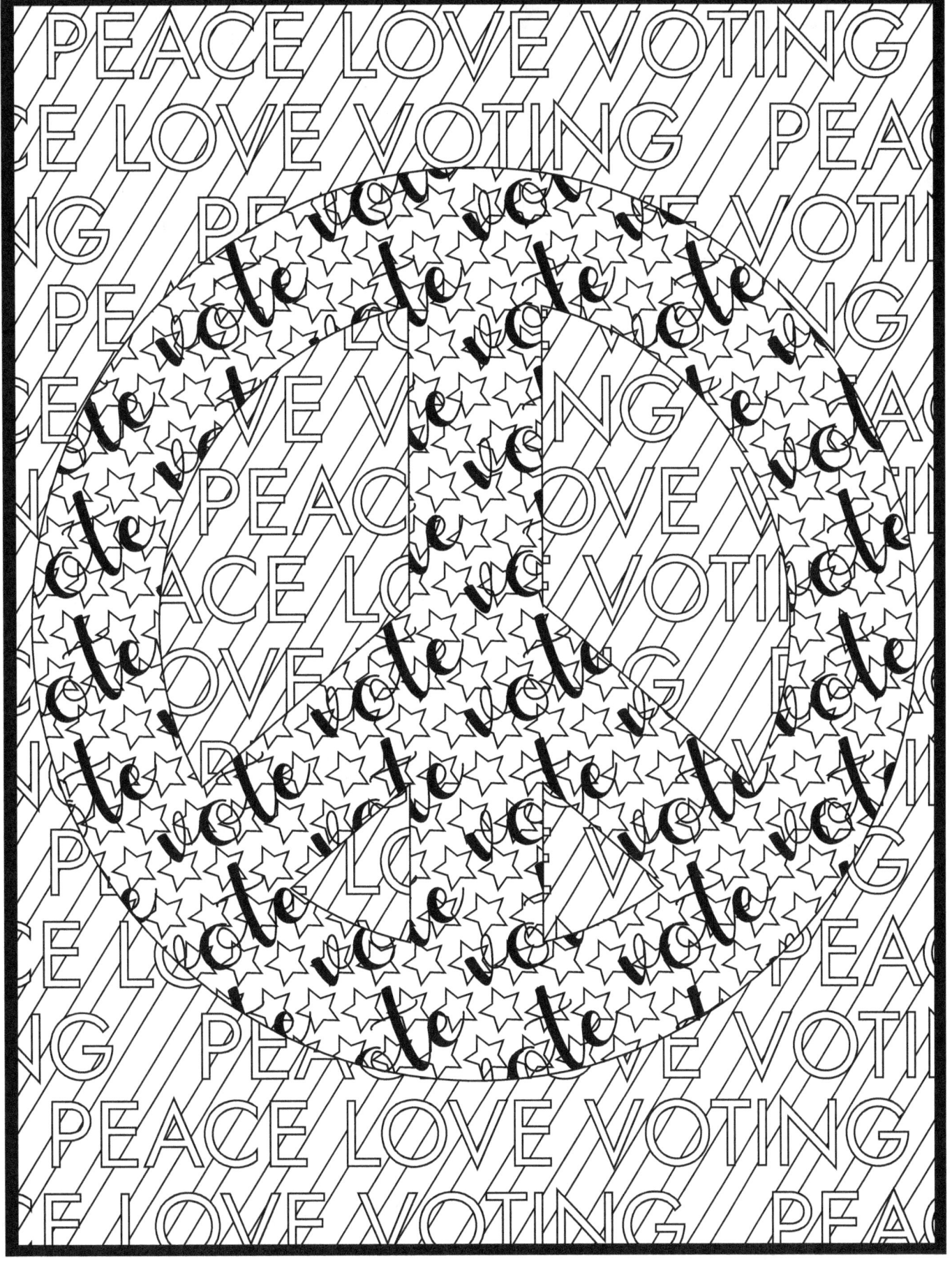

Peace, Love, and Voting

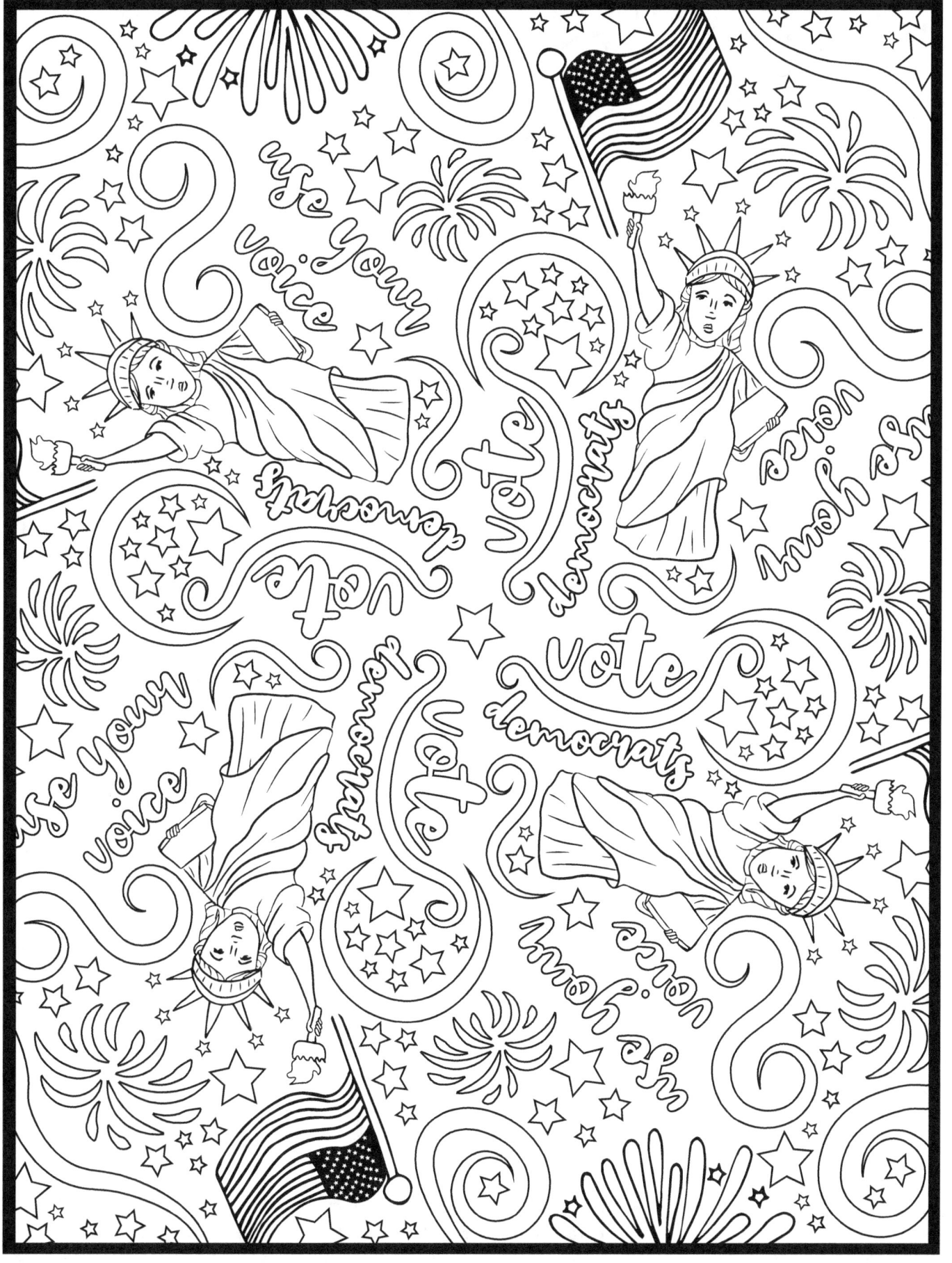

Liberty Mandala

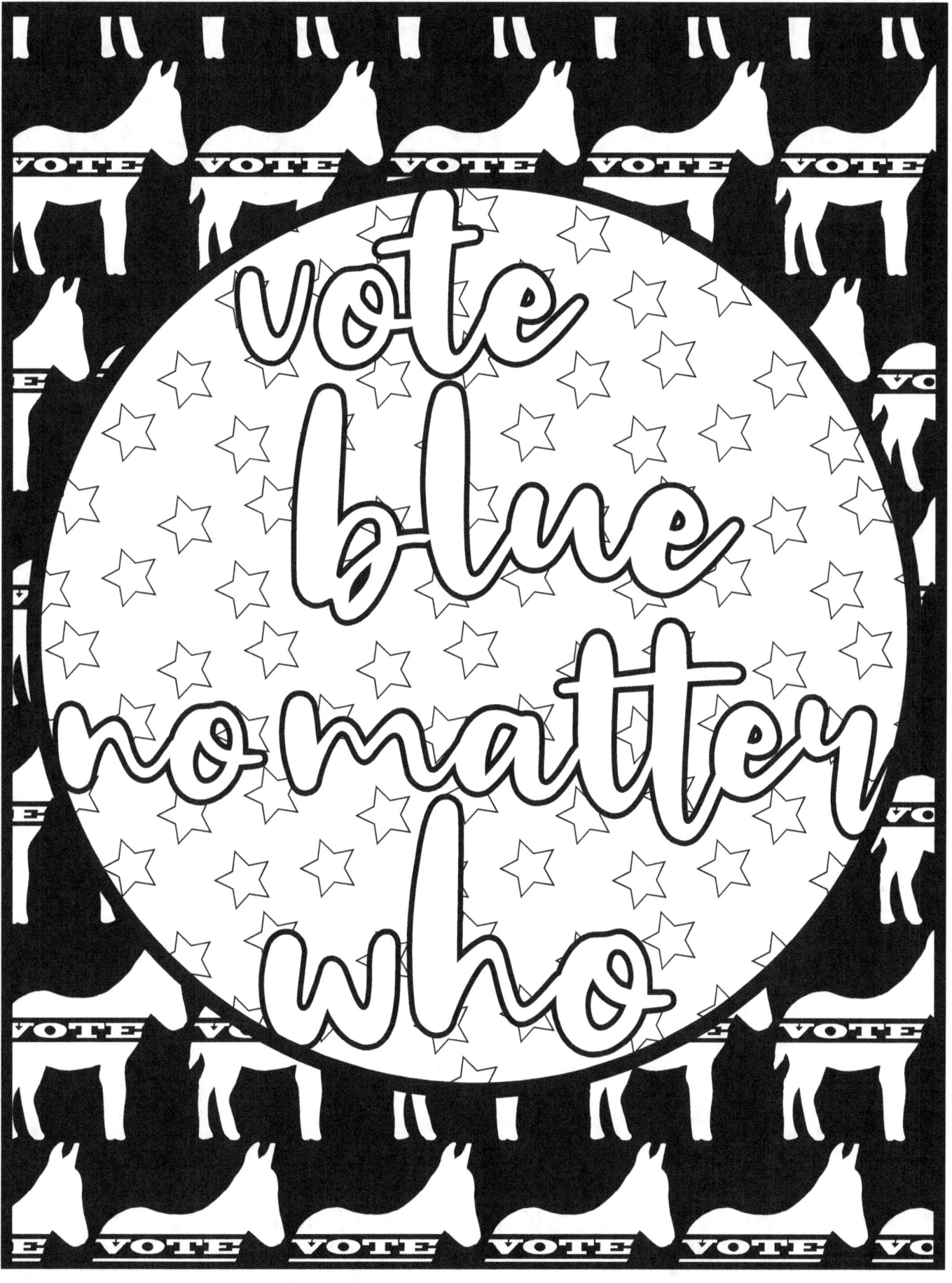

Vote blue no matter who

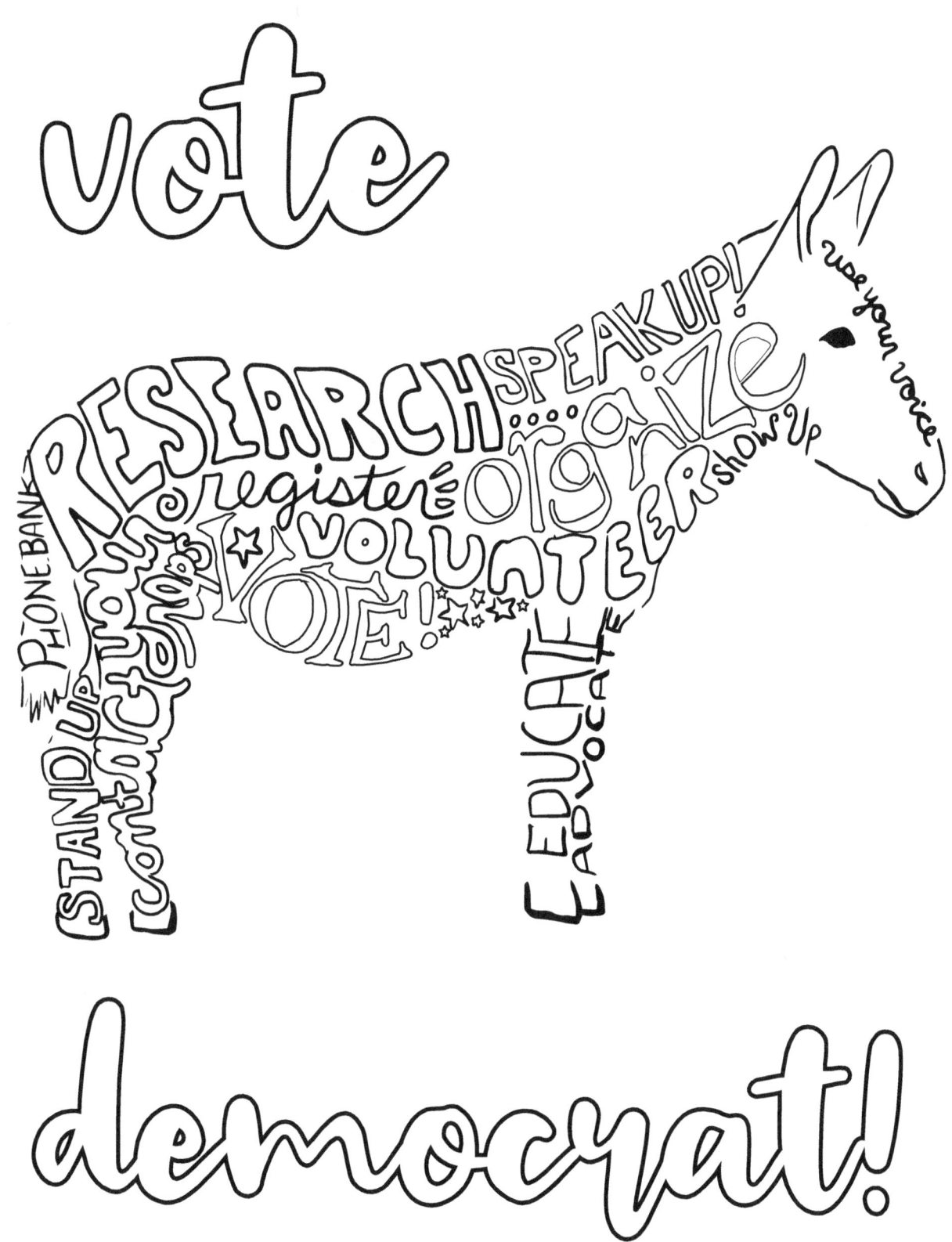

VOTE DEMOCRAT!

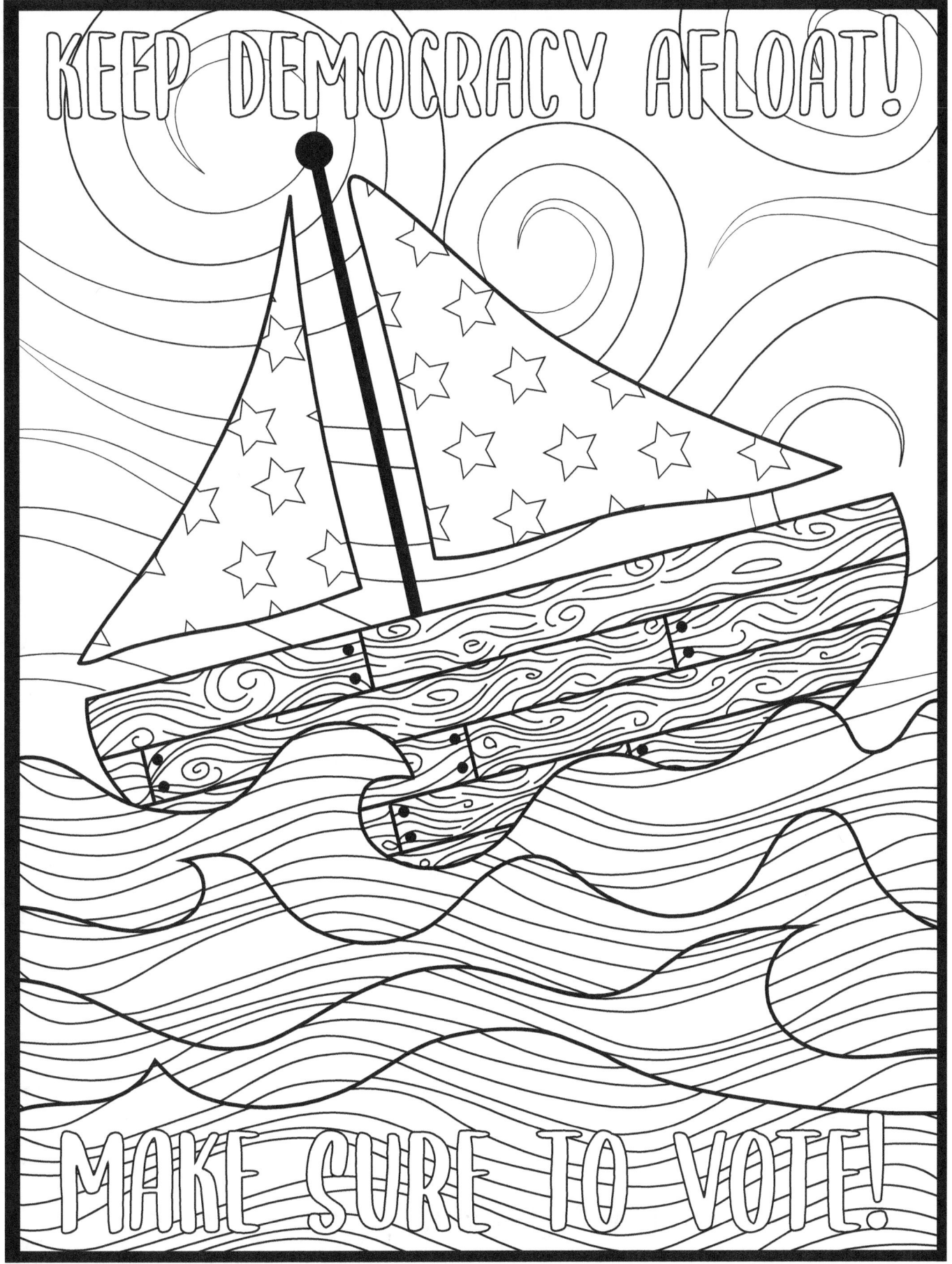

Keep democracy afloat

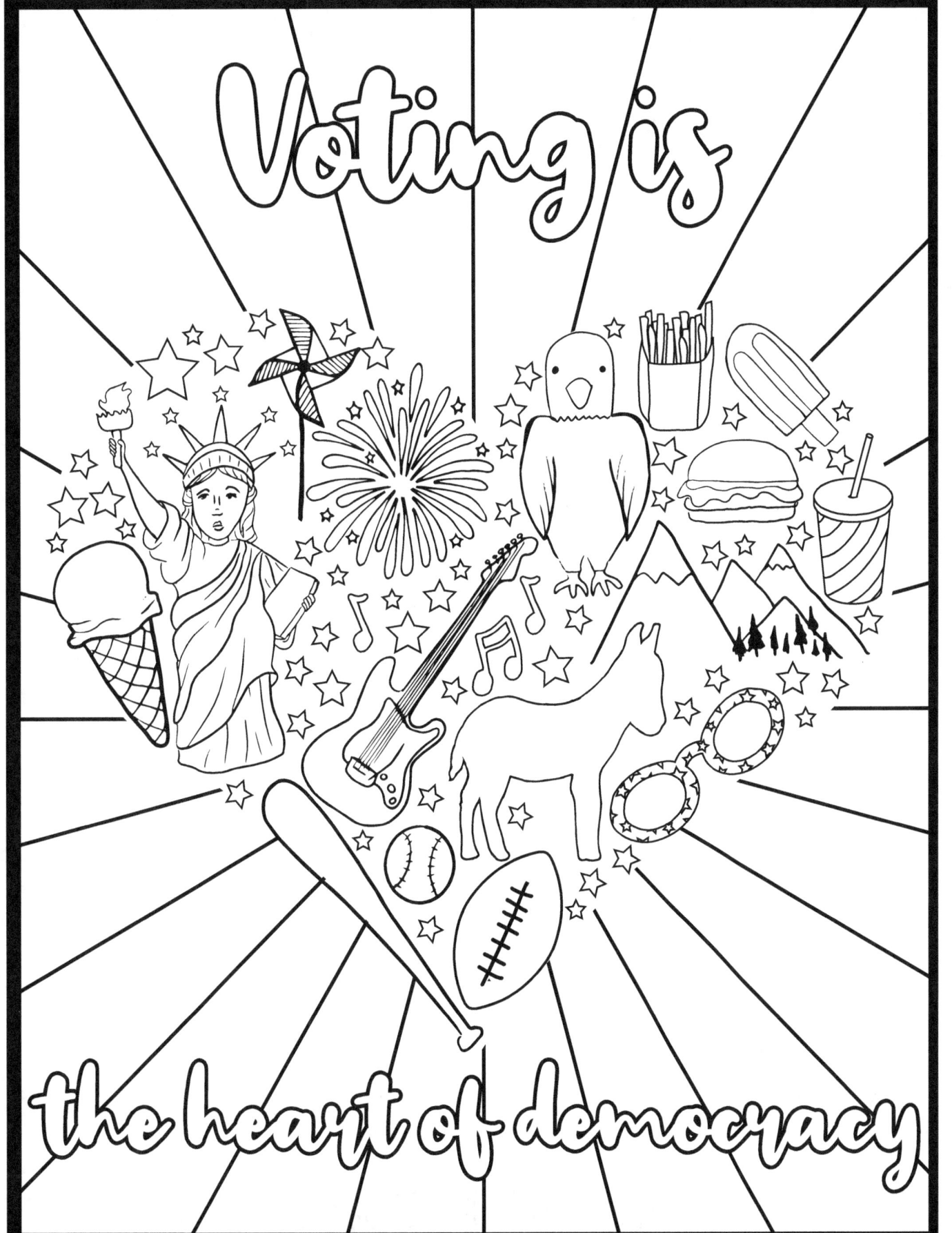

The heart of democracy

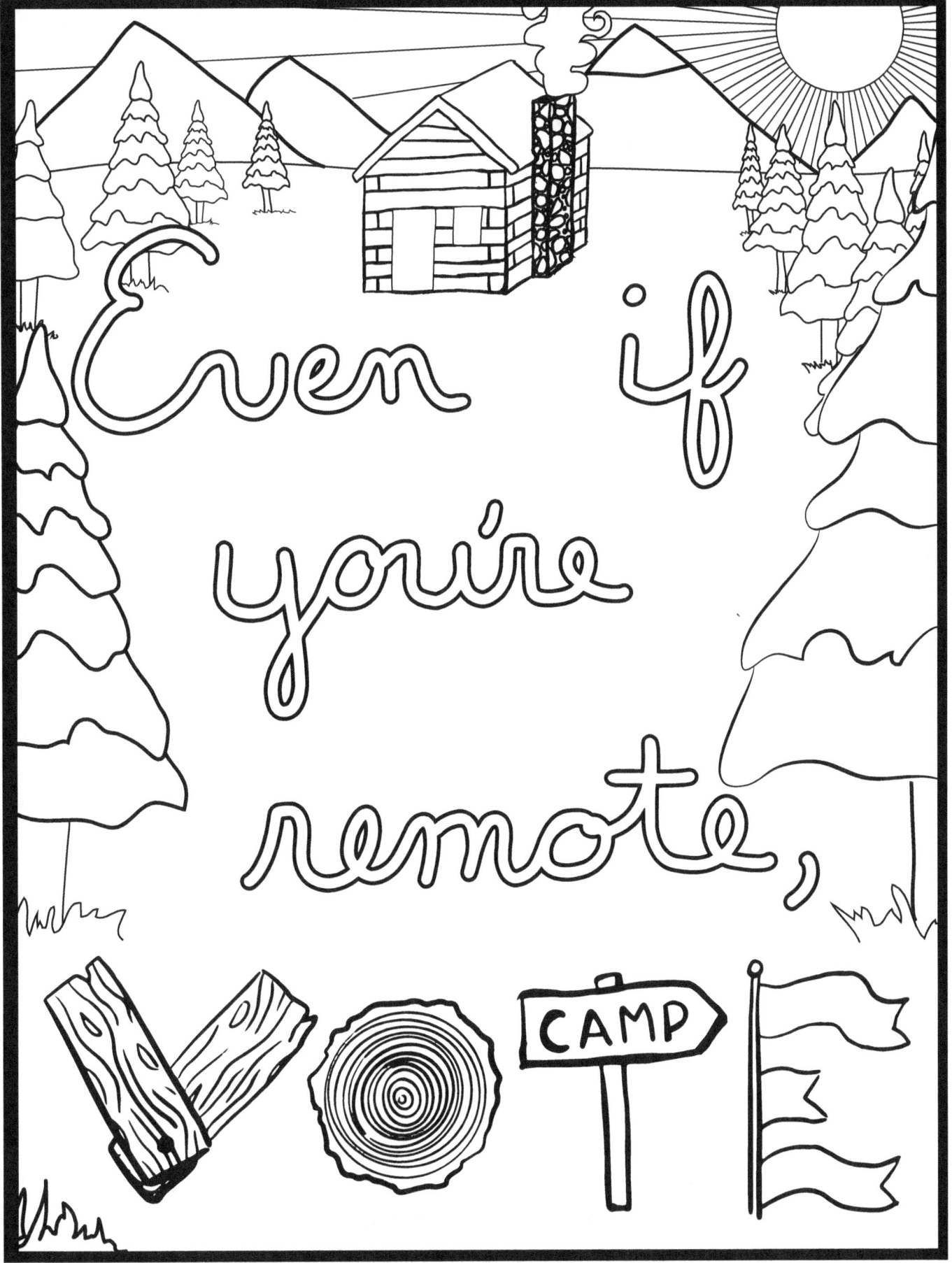

Remote Voting

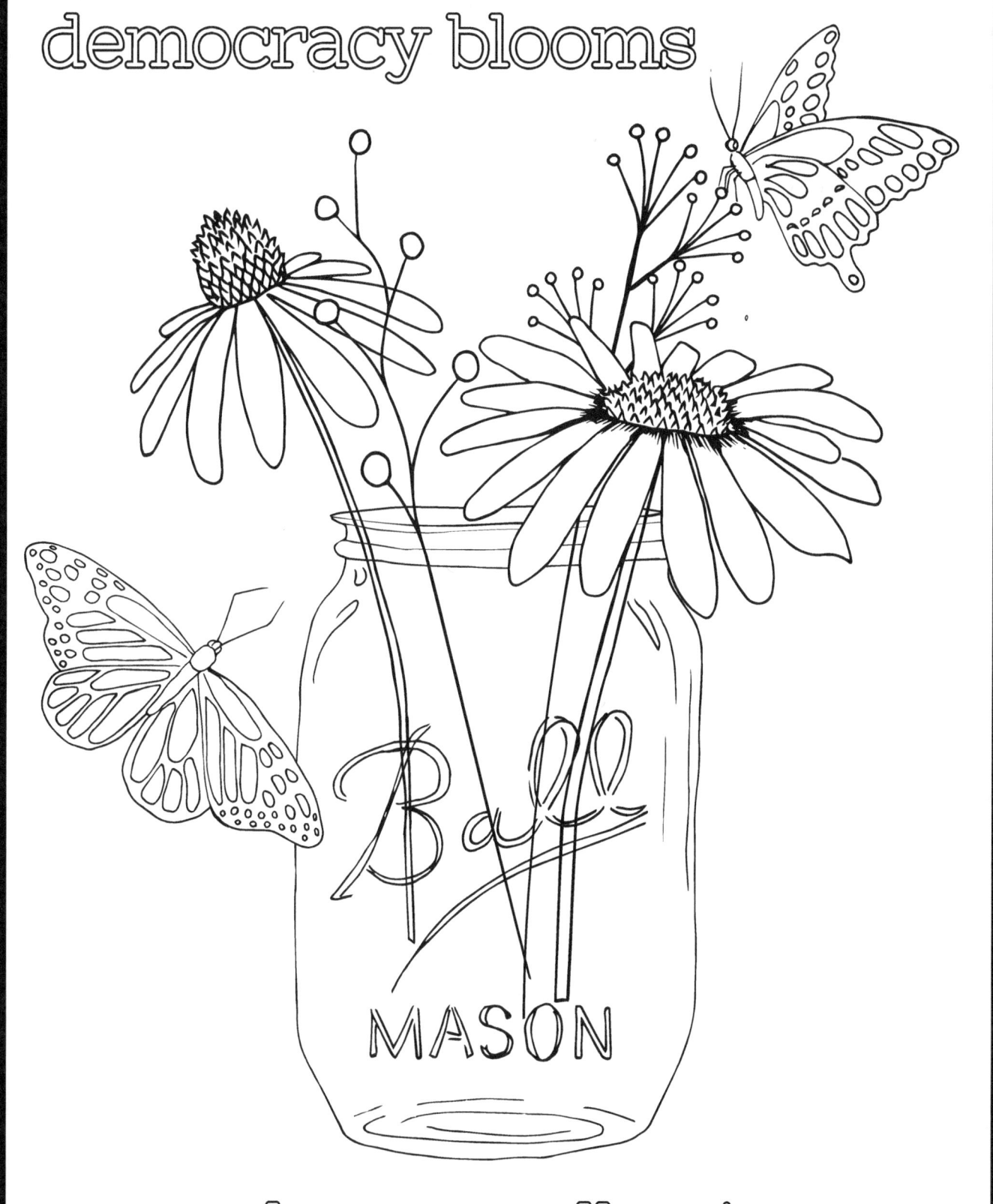

Democracy blooms

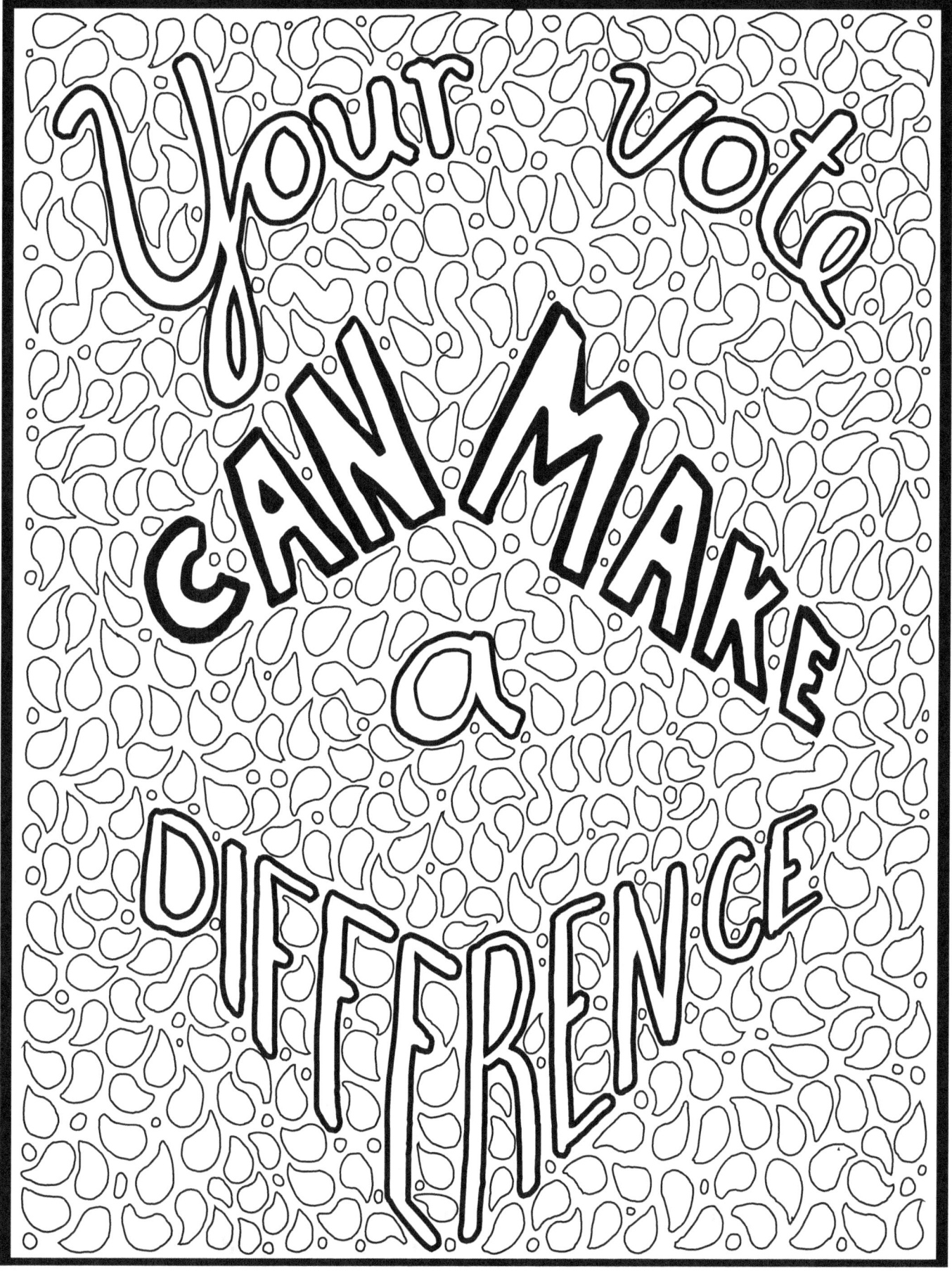

Your vote can make a difference

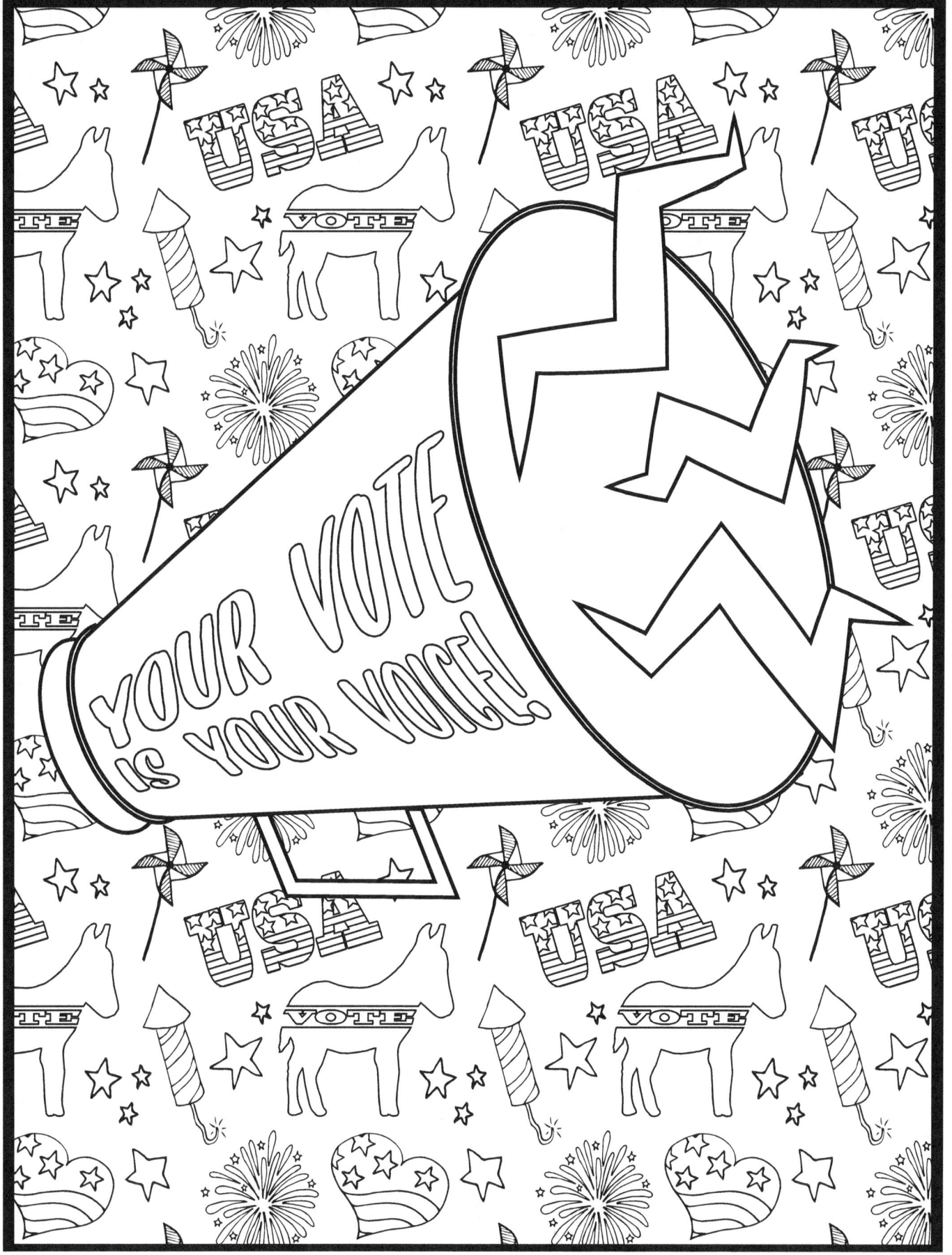

Your vote is your voice!